SYMPHONIES
Nos. 6 and 7
in Full Score

ANTONÍN DVOŘÁK

DOVER PUBLICATIONS, INC.
New York

Bibliographical Note

This Dover edition, first published in 1994, is an unabridged republication of two Dvořák symphonies, op. 60 and op. 70, originally published in separate volumes by N. Simrock, Berlin, as no. 1 [later called no. 6] and no. 2 [later called no. 7]. The original scores carry the following titles: [for Symphony No. 6]—*Symphonie (D dur) für grosses Orchester von Anton Dvořák. Op. 60. Partitur,* 1882; [for Symphony No. 7]—*Symphonie (No. 2, D moll) für grosses Orchester von Anton Dvořák. Op. 70. Partitur,* 1885. A table of contents and lists of instruments have been added to the Dover edition.

The publisher is grateful to the Eda Kuhn Loeb Music Library, Harvard University, for the loan of the original scores for reproduction.

Library of Congress Cataloging-in-Publication Data

Dvořák, Antonín, 1841–1904.
    [Symphonies, no. 6, op. 60, D major]
    Symphonies nos. 6 and 7 / Antonín Dvořák.—In full score.
    1 score.
    Reprint. 1st work originally published: Berlin : N. Simrock, 1882. 2nd work originally published: Berlin : N. Simrock, 1885.
    ISBN 0-486-28026-8
    1. Symphonies—Scores. I. Dvořák, Antonín, 1841–1904. Symphonies, no. 7, op. 70, D minor. 1994.
M1001.D97 no. 6 1994   94-19
                                                               CIP
                                                                M

Manufactured in the United States of America
Dover Publications, Inc., 31 East 2nd Street, Mineola, N.Y. 11501

CONTENTS

SYMPHONY No. 6
in D MAJOR, Op. 60

INSTRUMENTATION

2 Flutes [Flöten]
2 Oboes [Hoboen]
2 Clarinets (in A, B♭) [Clarinetten]
2 Bassoons [Fagotte]

4 Horns (in D, E, F, B♭ Bass) [Hörner]
2 Trumpets (in D, B♭) [Trompeten]
3 Trombones [Posaunen]
Tuba [Tuba]

Timpani [Pauken]

Violins I, II [Violine]
Violas [Bratsche]
Cellos [Violoncell.]
Basses [Contrabass]

I.

Symphony No. 6 (I)   49

II.

III.
Scherzo (Furiant)

IV.
Finale

SYMPHONY No. 7
in D MINOR, Op. 70

INSTRUMENTATION

2 Flutes [Flöten]
2 Oboes [Hoboen]
2 Clarinets (in A, B♭) [Clarinetten]
2 Bassoons [Fagotte]

4 Horns (in D, F) [Hörner]
2 Trumpets (in C, D, F) [Trompeten]
3 Trombones [Posaunen]

Timpani [Pauken]

Violins I, II [Violine]
Violas [Bratsche]
Cellos [Violoncell.]
Basses [Bass]

I.

II.

III.
Scherzo

IV.
Finale

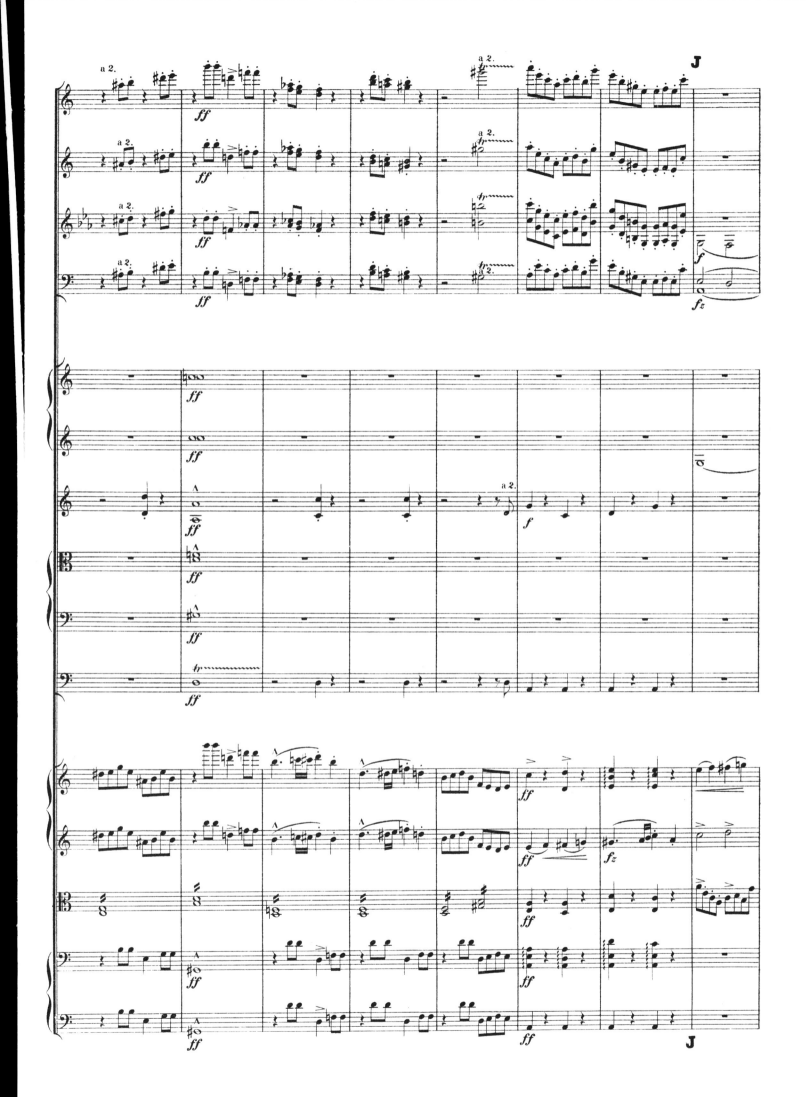

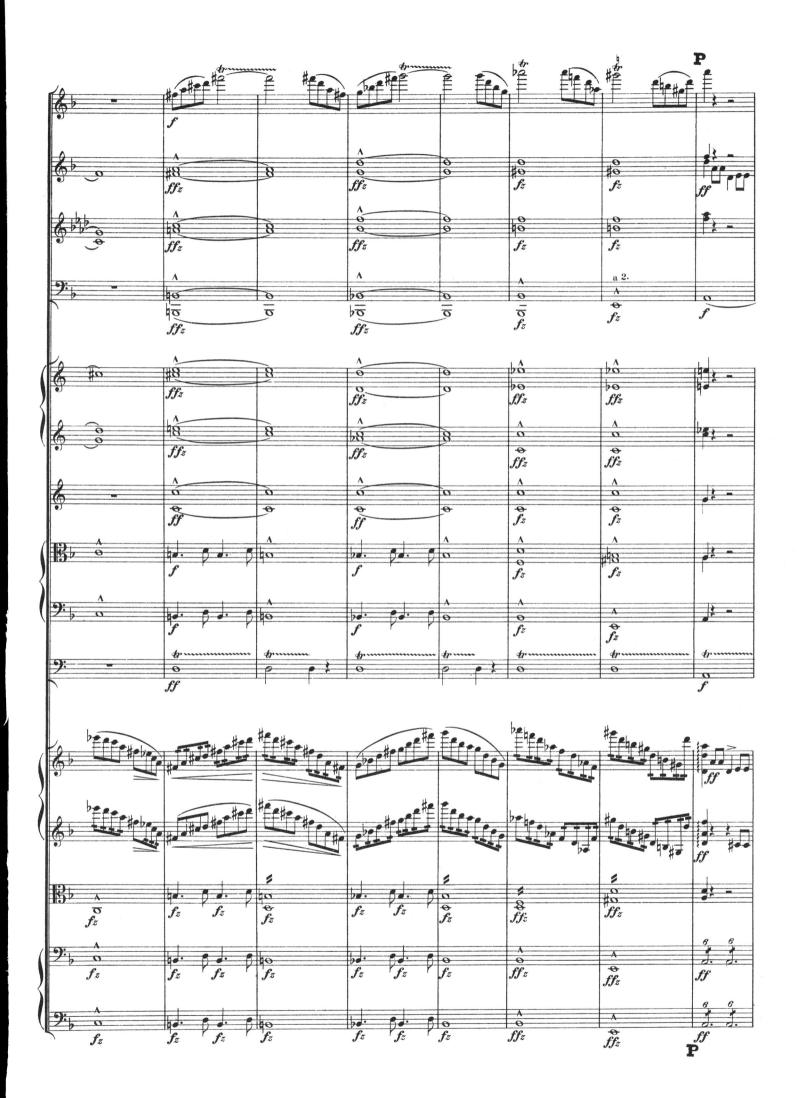